Walk, Run, Skip, and Jump!

Daniel Faraday

I0806969

Rosen Readers

Rosen Classroom™

New York

Published in 2013 by The Rosen Publishing Group, Inc.
29 East 21st Street, New York, NY 10010

Book Design: Michael Harmon

Photo Credits: Cover Monkey Business Images/Shutterstock.com; p. 5 © iStockphoto.com/LeggNet; p. 7 BestPhotoByMonikaGniot/Shutterstock.com; p. 9 Konstantin Sutyagin/Shutterstock.com; p. 11 Nagy-Bagoly Arpad/Shutterstock.com; p. 13 © iStockphoto.com/aabejon; p. 15 (boy) michaeljung/Shutterstock.com; p. 15 (background) majeczka/Shutterstock.com.

ISBN: 978-1-4488-8680-7
6-pack ISBN: 978-1-4488-8681-4

Manufactured in the United States of America

CPSIA Compliance Information: Batch #WS12RC: For further information contact Rosen Publishing, New York, New York at 1-800-237-9932.

Word Count: 12

Contents

Pat walks.

Pam runs.

Tim runs.

Tom skips.

Jill skips.

Will jumps.

Words to Know

jump

run

skip

walk

Index